MW01259749

San Juan Bonanza

The majestic, beautiful San Juan Mountains have challenged all who come within the sphere of their seven 10,000-foot passes and a dozen 14,000-foot peaks, 23 percent of Colorado's fourteeners.

SAN JUAN BONANZA

Western Colorado's Mining Legacy

JOHN L. NINNEMANN

DUANE A. SMITH

UNIVERSITY OF NEW MEXICO PRESS ~ ALBUQUERQUE

YEAR   PRINTING
10 09 08 07 06   1 2 3 4 5

LIBRARY OF CONGRESS CATALOGING-IN-PUBLICATION DATA

Smith, Duane A.
     San Juan bonanza : western Colorado's mining legacy /
Duane A. Smith, John L. Ninnemann.
               p. cm.
     ISBN-13: 978-0-8263-3578-4 (cloth : alk. paper)
     ISBN-10: 0-8263-3578-0 (cloth : alk. paper)
1. San Juan Mountains Region (Colo. and N.M.)—History.
2. San Juan Mountains Region (Colo. and N.M.)—History—Pictorial works.
3. Mining districts—San Juan Mountains Region (Colo. and N.M.)—History.
4. Mining districts—San Juan Mountains Region (Colo. and N.M.)—History—Pictorial works.
5. Mines and mineral resources—San Juan Mountains Region (Colo. and N.M.)—History.
6. Gold mines and mining—San Juan Mountains Region (Colo. and N.M.)—History.
7. Silver mines and mining—San Juan Mountains Region (Colo. and N.M.)—History.
8. Mining camps—San Juan Mountains Region (Colo. and N.M.)—History.
9. Frontier and pioneer life—San Juan Mountains Region.
I. Ninnemann, John L. II. Title.
     F782.S19S64 2006
     978.8'3—dc22

                                        2005025894

book and jacket design and type composition: Kathleen Sparkes
all photographs by John L. Ninnemann

Printed in China by Everbest Printing Company, Ltd.

to Glen Crandall

Our good friend and
fellow back-road explorer

CONTENTS

PROLOGUE   ix

    MAP OF THE SAN JUANS   XV

THE ARRIVAL OF THE MINERS   1

SAN JUAN URBANIZATION   47

EPILOGUE   75

INDEX   83

*The rugged, beautiful, sky-touching San Juans—the visitor's joy,
the miner's bane—await the oncoming winter on a warm fall day.
The remains of the Tomboy Mine sit at the upper left.*

PROLOGUE

THE SAN JUAN MOUNTAINS OFFER A FASCINATING HISTORY TO THE interested student or visitor. For five hundred years the summer home of the Utes, explored, named, and mined by the Spanish 250 years ago, and 150 years ago opened and permanently settled by European Americans, the San Juans are the saga of the West, locked high in one of the most beautiful and rugged mountain ranges in the United States. Much of what remains of yesteryear, however, stands in lonely peace, monuments to days gone by.

The promise of gold and silver enticed Europeans and Americans to prospect in the San Juans. Dreams became reality with the 1859 Pikes Peak gold rush, which brought prospectors and miners to the central Rockies. The evolution of interest in the San Juans can be seen in the following reports. United States Commissioner of Mining Statistics Rossiter Raymond wrote in 1869:

> The western half of Colorado is not much known beyond
> fifty miles from the mountain range, though several parties
> of prospectors have explored the country at different times.
> Some placers and veins have been found but no mining has
> been done on a large scale, except in the Snake River district,
> far east of the San Juans.

In 1873 Raymond discussed the "new" San Juan country:

> The mines are located in Baker's Park [Silverton], on the
> headwaters of the Las Animas, a tributary of the San Juan
> River. The country is accessible with some difficulty by way
> of Pueblo Del Norte and from there up the Rio Grande to

The north edge of the San Juans from Dallas Divide, where once the Rio Grande
Southern chugged past. It is easy to see why the railroad advertised itself as the
"Silver San Juan Scenic Line." Finished in 1891, it connected Durango with Ridgway.

the divide, which has to be crossed into Baker's Park. Some
of the mines, such as the Little Giant, are spoken of as rich
gold-veins, while the great majority are lead-veins, rich in
silver. The coming summer will probably witness great
activity in the San Juan Country. I have no doubt smelting-
works will be erected there.

Several summers later (1880), Colorado reporter and writer Frank
Fossett described the individual counties in the San Juans and their
prospects. Yet amid the dreams of wealth, Fossett noted

These mountains (San Juans) contain thousands of silver
veins, many of them of huge size, and some of great richness.

There are also gold lodes and placers. . . . The rugged and
almost impassable character of the mountains and their vast
extent, and the heavy snows and long winters, have acted
as serious drawbacks to growth and development. There is
probably more country standing on edge in this section
than anywhere else beneath the sun.

The land still "stands on edge," and the dreams still float around the
mountains and down the canyons and vanish, swirling about the valleys.
Once those dreams moved men to search and dig, live and love. Now the
silent, wind-haunted remains dimly remind visitors of what once was in
a land where tomorrow did not exist.

Once people were here, with high hopes and dreams about the future of the Red Mountain district. Now all that remains are weathered boards and rusting machinery. Annie Rogers, who lived in the district in the early 1890s, remembered it as "a glorious country in summer and majestic in winter."

That silence speaks volumes of what was and what might have been. In the words of the poet Thomas Hornsby Ferril:

I've come to this lovely valley
In quest of peace of mind,
I want to wander these lost towns
Where not a house still stands.

—"Report of My Strange Encounter
with Lily Bull-Domingo"

Colorado has many state emblems but none prettier than the columbine found throughout the mountains.

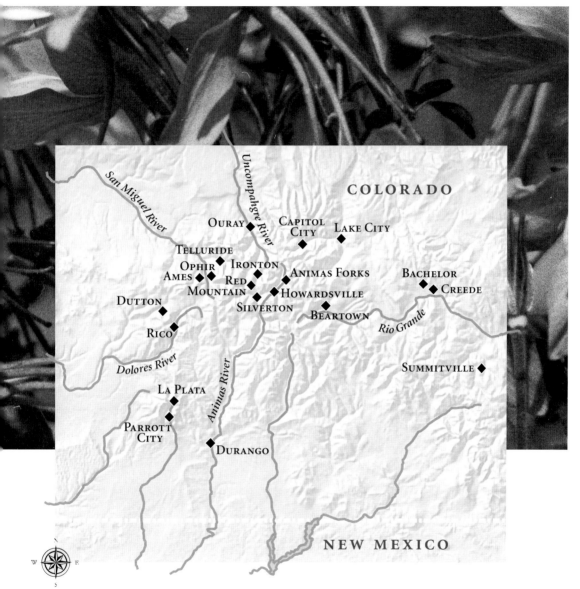

COLORADO

San Miguel River

Uncompahgre River

OURAY ◆   CAPITOL
              CITY   LAKE CITY
                  ◆   ◆

TELLURIDE
◆   IRONTON
OPHIR ◆   ◆
AMES ◆ RED   ◆   ANIMAS FORKS   BACHELOR
◆ ◆ MOUNTAIN ◆   ◆   ◆
                HOWARDSVILLE   ◆ CREEDE
DUTTON   ◆ SILVERTON
   ◆   BEARTOWN
RICO   ◆   *Rio Grande*
◆

Dolores River

LA PLATA   SUMMITVILLE
◆   ◆

Animas River

PARROTT
CITY
◆
     ◆ DURANGO

NEW MEXICO

San Juan Mining Region 1860–1914

Poet and miner Alfred King wrote, "Wherever I wander,
my spirit still dwells, in the Silvery San Juan."
The photo shows La Plata Mountains, in King's words,
in "winter's immaculate mantle of white."

THE ARRIVAL OF THE MINERS

~~~~~~

By and by I was smitten with silver fever. "Prospecting parties" were leaving for the mountains every day, and discovering and taking possession of rich silver-bearing lodes and ledges of quartz. Plainly this was the road to fortune.

I would have been more or less than human if I had not gone mad like the rest.

I succumbed and grew as frenzied as the craziest.

I confess, without shame, that I expected to find masses of silver lying all about the ground. I expected to see it glittering in the sun on the mountain summits. I said nothing about this, for some instinct told me that I might possibly have an exaggerated idea about it. . . .

THUS CONFESSED A NOVICE NEVADA MINER, ONE SAMUEL CLEMENS, in the 1860s. Better than any San Juaner of a decade later, he tried to describe "silver fever" or "gold fever" to the uninitiated. Even in his "frenzy," Clemens understood, somewhere in the deep recesses of his excitement, that he held to "exaggerated" expectations. He was right and so too were the miners in the generation that followed as they despaired about why they had ever left home to "get rich without working."

Long before the late nineteenth century, prospectors and miners had been drawn to the San Juan Mountains. Wandering around those majestic mountains, canyons, and high valleys, they imagined them to be the "mother lode," whence all gold and silver came.

A forlorn boiler sits on the edge of Hurricane Pass, looking down into California Gulch. It was not always this way. The Engineering and Mining Journal *(July 12, 1890) noted, "San Juan mines never before looked as promising as at the present time."*

To capture that treasure would take some doing. To mine in the San Juans meant living, climbing, and working in the highest mining region in the United States, arguably the most rugged as well. Add to this the fickle weather, which generated snow and cold any month of the year, and the problems magnify. As an old miner declared, the climate produced three months of mighty late fall and nine months "of damn hard winter." To match nature alone would take a strong measure of stamina and a never-say-die spirit. Then came the mining problems, the transportation difficulties, the financial shortfalls, the smelting dilemmas, and the isolation.

Why would people tackle such obstacles? They believed. They believed that somewhere in these mountainous depths they would somehow find their "promised land." They had optimistic, enthusiastic faith—and faith, it is said, can move mountains. "What made them go was a sort of urge, a frame of mind," David Lavender later wrote in *Red Mountain*, his story of the San Juan district.

That frame of mind put one man to work as a miner, another as a merchant, and another as a lawyer. It brought in their wives and sweethearts and single women as homemakers, teachers, boardinghouse operators, and dance hall girls. Some stayed, more left, but in some way, they all contributed to life in the San Juans.

The Spanish arrived in the San Juans first. Certainly by the 1760s, they knew this land. Exactly when they came is not known, but the initial tiny settlements scattered along the Rio Grande were not that far away from the San Juans, and the Spanish had been searching for gold and silver almost from the day Columbus reached the New World in 1492.

When Juan de Rivera led a party into the Plata Mountains in 1765, he wrote his report about the region as if he expected his readers to be somewhat knowledgeable about the places he described. Further, when the Domquez/Escalante expedition passed by the mountains in 1776, Escalante noted in his journal: "They say there are veins and outcroppings of metal. . . . The opinion formed previously by some persons from the accounts of

David Lavender's novel Red Mountain *tells the story of the Red Mountain district and mines like this one. "You've never been at Red Mountain. Three peaks on fire, I tell you. Mineral in every fissure."*

various Indians and of some citizens of this kingdom that they were silver mines caused the mountain to be called Sierra de la Plata."

These New Mexicans prospected and mined despite the region's isolation and sometimes unfriendly Utes. They did so in somewhat of a clandestine manner, because they did not want to have to give the king or his agents the king's "royal fifth" of what they found. Thus they left behind names—Animas, La Plata, San Juan, Dolores—and many legends of lost mines and buried treasure. The legends must have been New Mexican since the inhabitants of the San Juan region then, the Utes, did not mine.

That these folk once worked there, dreaming of great wealth, was discovered by those who came long afterward. Mine workings, Spanish coins, and old tools found in the 1870s proved the Spanish had labored among the mountains. Meanwhile, beckoning legends drifted through the San Juans like the wind. No one really knew whence they came or where the legendary mines might be found, but these mines promised much for the lucky finder. Probably many of the lost "mines," sometimes nothing more

Lake Como, where Spanish miners reportedly once worked. Starting in the 1760s, stories of minerals in these mountains beckoned others to come. The men left behind legends of lost mines and buried treasure and melodious names for the mountains and streams.

THE ARRIVAL OF
THE MINERS

The trail to the North Star Mine on King Solomon Mountain, where men's dreams soared as high as its 12,800-foot elevation. Mining engineer Eben Olcott worked there in the early 1880s. "The trail up here ascends 4,200 feet in not over 3 miles and lies along the edge of precipices."

than mere dents in the ground, were found, relocated, and mined without their new owners realizing what had transpired.

By the opening of the nineteenth century, as Spanish power and influence waned throughout the Americas, the San Juans, on the far isolated rim of the empire, ebbed from interest, if not from memory. Then the Mexican people rose up and threw off their Spanish rulers, and New Mexico became part of Mexico. This hardly made a grand impact on the settlers in the Rio Grande Valley and none whatsoever on the Utes, who still roamed freely in the mountains and valleys.

The Mexican government made a mistake, understandable neverthe-less, in opening the Southwest to people in the United States. The Spanish authorities had encountered great difficulty in getting Spanish settlers to move into Texas and beyond, but Yankees appeared willing to take the risk. On they came to California, New Mexico, and Texas to settle, to Santa Fe to trade, and into the mountains' vastness to trap beaver. The result was almost predictable where the Yankees went—the flag soon followed. Texas fell first. Then, following the Mexican War, all this land, from part of the Wyoming-Colorado border to Arizona and California to Texas, became part of the United States.

At the same time as negotiations were taking place to end that war, in 1848, in distant California, James Marshall discovered gold on the south fork of the American River. That set off a gold rush that changed Ameri-can history and had an impact on much of the world as excited people rushed to the new Eldorado. Ten years later, in 1858, another gold strike set off a second rush to the Pikes Peak country. The rush of 1859 focused primarily on prospects east of the Continental Divide, miles and moun-tains from the San Juans. Yet golden visions and, yes, greed bestir a drive in men's and women's souls.

Within a year, prospectors entered the lofty recesses of the isolated San Juans. So proved the lure of gold on the newly arrived Coloradans' minds. Prospector/promoter Charles Baker journeyed via Abiquiu, New Mexico, and then north up the Animas River into the heart of the moun-tains. The park where he ventured soon took his name and would even-tually be home to Silverton.

By that mysterious, always-humming mining camp "telegraph," word of a bonanza soon reached eastward. Baker helped it along with letters to the *Rocky Mountain News*. A mini-rush arrived in 1861 as prospectors scrambled to get in on the ground floor. Baker stood ready, with a road from Abiquiu to the mines, a town platted to the south in the more hospitable lower Animas Valley (Animas City), and an organized mining district. With one swoop, he cornered the ways to make wealth in a min-ing rush—a toll road, real estate sales, a proclaimed bonanza, and a bit of mining along the way.

It all came to naught. Little gold was found, the recently arrived San Juaners cussed Baker roundly, and the rushers rushed back to civilization. *News* editor William Byers called it a "humbug," which it nearly was, and the San Juans returned to peace and quiet. This first San Juan gold fever failed for a variety of reasons: isolation, the threat of the Utes (whose land the miners overran), the onrushing Civil War back in the States (which caused federal troops to be withdrawn from the territory), and most of all the lack of rich diggings.

A mine portal near Animas Forks.
Mark Twain is quoted as saying,
"A mine is a hole in the ground owned
by a liar." In any case, such scoundrels
practiced their art in the San Juans, and
gullible or greedy investors fell victim.

The dreams did not die after that bleak summer of '61. Still the legends of lost Spanish mines, which may have attracted Baker in the first place, floated around. Some gold, if not much, had been found. Might there be more? Obviously other parts of the Colorado mountains held gold deposits, and by the end of the war, silver joined the excitement, so why not the San Juans?

The years rolled by, and the Civil War ground to its costly end while Colorado languished. The territory, with a tarnished reputation from mining stock speculation and busted mines, had neither the experience, the finances, nor the equipment to handle the complex ores that had been found. But Coloradans don't give up.

Back came the prospectors in the summer of '69, up the Dolores River to near where the town of Rico one day would be. Then the next year parties prospected both there and in Baker's Park. They staked mines and opened "million-dollar" mines but only stayed during the warmer seasons. As soon as snow flew, they flew. But the word was out again and despite Byers's protests of "humbug," the San Juans generated excitement once more. By the spring of 1872, the rush launched into full swing.

The worried Utes looked on and protested to their agent. He in turn protested to Washington about the intruders trespassing on reservation land, and Uncle Sam found himself caught between vocal voters and upset Utes. Washington was faced with a lose-lose situation.

Mining and all that came with it promised to develop southwestern Colorado's natural resources and bring settlement to this lofty "wilderness." That defined America's "Manifest Destiny"—to develop the West, utilize its natural resources, bring civilization to one and all, and multiply America's power and prestige. All of that, though, begged the question with the Utes. This, after all, had been their homeland for several centuries, and the land had been guaranteed to them by a series of treaties. They did not take kindly to these intruders. Fortunately, however, warfare did not break out as it had, and would, elsewhere.

The prospectors, and now the miners, wanted the Utes out as badly as the miners wanted to stay. They could protest too and did. Who better to develop and disseminate San Juan wealth than these stalwart San Juan pioneers who challenged the mountains and matched the isolation to open the trails and mines and exploit the mineral wealth? Even down in the Animas Valley, farmers and ranchers started to stake out their own agricultural bonanza to tap the mining trade. The Utes saw no benefit in all this, and experience had taught them that their way of life would disappear before the hoe, plow, pan, pick, and shovel.

Washington, caught in a pressure-filled bind, first ordered the intruders out by June 1, 1873. Predictably howls of protest rose from angered

San Juaners, territorial newspapers, and politicians in Denver. A vacillating Washington caved in, and President Ulysses Grant indefinitely suspended the obnoxious order.

Coloradans generally decided the Ute reservation was far too large and mounted a campaign to settle the Ute "question." No "question" existed with the Utes—they wanted to stay. Washington decided to do what it did best: send out a commission, headed by the skilled diplomat and president of the Board of Indian Commissioners, Felix Brunot. A week's negotiations in September 1873 produced the Brunot agreement and found the Utes ceding four million acres of mining land (the entire San Juans) for an annual payment of $25,000.

In the amazingly but typically fast-moving mining West, the miners in four years had received virtually all they sought. Utes, however, still lived north, south, and west of the mines. That caused some distress when the miners continued to trespass on Ute land. Protests mounted from both sides and the call "the Utes must go" bounced around the mountains and throughout the territory.

Not that Animas Forks witnessed much crime, but it had a jail ready.
More likely, it helped sober those suffering from a "San Juan" head.
Whiskey at ten thousand feet could produce a fast "head."

A lonesome claim marker tells of silver aspirations never fulfilled. No excavation or dump exists nearby on King Solomon Mountain to show that anything came of this claim. A lode claim such as this one could have a maximum size of six hundred by fifteen hundred feet.

Even though the Ute question had not been resolved to Coloradans' complete satisfaction, 1873 marked a pivotal year for the San Juans. These mountains, or the "Eldorado," that promised land of wealth, had been opened, immigration grew, primitive paths had at least become primitive trails, and once again the region was known abroad. Gold might have brought prospectors, but now silver mines captured their attention. Some prospectors were even thinking of developing permanent mining camps for year-round operation, joining the farmers down in the Animas Valley. In economically depressed Colorado, the San Juans became the hot spot. By the end of the year, embryo mining camps nestled in river valleys and parks and along mountainsides. Permanent settlement had come to stay.

Land could now be claimed, legally purchased, and sold without trespassing on Ute land. Mining districts had been organized and mining laws established, giving the prospector, miner, and outside capitalist a legal opportunity to stake a claim, open a mine, and buy one with a margin of safety.

Still investors did not come. These were not "poor man's" diggings, where a pan and a shovel might turn up a fortune. It took money to make money once miners had blasted into the San Juans' granite depths. It also took skill to recognize the ore-bearing rock, trace the mineralized vein

The Arrival of

the Miners

to stake a claim, timber the portal, and tunnel into the mountain. Nor did miners have a smelter available to work the complex silver and gold ore. What reduction works they had often proved nearly worthless. The mineral treasure box of the San Juans contained many minerals—copper, lead, and zinc, to name a few—as well as sulfur and other less desirable ones. Transportation problems continued to limit development, and winter weather cut the region off from the outside world.

Then came the national crash of 1873 with the following depression, which hung on depressingly for years in the young territory and in its even younger San Juan mining region. Prospecting continued, mining continued, but the times raged against them. By 1877, with matters starting to improve, hopes soared once more. Maybe now investors would come, skilled smelter men would venture into the district, and transportation

Danger does exist in old mines, although this portal has been gated to all but small animals.

would be solved by the coming of that all-American nineteenth-century favorite, the railroad.

It might have transpired just like that, but something happened on the way to the promised land. That something was Leadville, Colorado's greatest silver district, which exploded on the scene in that wonderful year of 1878. Investors fell all over themselves to invest in Leadville, and the railroads raced and fought to tap this silver bonanza. For the first time, but not the last, the San Juans remained a bridesmaid, not the bride.

By the mid-1880s, the San Juans appeared to be rebounding from the Leadville setback. Then Aspen buoyantly proclaimed itself Colorado's new "silver queen." Again the San Juans receded, but their day was coming.

Leadville ushered in Colorado's silver era. Silver might have been found earlier at Georgetown, Caribou, in the San Juans, and a few other scattered places. But none of them matched Leadville, which seemingly made millionaires overnight and challenged Denver as Colorado's greatest city. There was even talk of making it the state's capital. Colorado had become the centennial state back in 1876, the year that marked the nation's one hundred years of independence.

Ore wagons and, perhaps later, trucks once waited here for a load of ore to be taken to a nearby mill or smelter.

| THE ARRIVAL OF
THE MINERS

*At one time considered "a device to lead mortal souls to hell," the railroad
proved the savior of the San Juans and other mining districts as well.
When the railroad arrived, the region finally boomed. Every major San
Juan district gained the iron horse, which carried equipment, investors,
and almost everything else needed.*

The San Juans had celebrated that anniversary appropriately and
looked ahead toward a more promising tomorrow. It now seemed that all
had been delayed, maybe indefinitely. Then a faint light glimmered fitfully
in the gloom. The Denver & Rio Grande, amid its rush to Leadville, also
planned to come farther west to tap the potential that existed in the San
Juans. At least a small measure of hope could be resurrected—and it
would prove more than a small measure.

Colorado's homegrown "baby" railroad, having adopted the three-
foot narrow gauge, which proved perfect for mountain railroading, raced
to as many of Colorado's booming silver districts as possible. In 1879–80
survey crews worked on finding a route along the Animas River and
through its precipitous canyon, then on to Baker's Park and Silverton.
Silverton could hardly wait for the arrival of the iron horse. The "Gem
of the Rockies," as the camp liked to refer to itself, understood the significance of it all.

Railroading in the San Juans tested the knowledge of engineers and construction crews. The famous Corkscrew Gulch Turntable allowed Otto Mears's Silverton Railroad to reach Ironton. Faced with a narrow, steep section of track, the fifty-foot turntable, plus a Y, allowed engines to be turned around and then to be recoupled with the cars that had been rolled through the table.

La Plata Miner (December 24, 1881) stressed that the D&RG's approach would "give us needed facilities" of both transportation and reduction works: "Our miners would no longer seek to induce capitalists to purchase prospects." The miners would work the prospects and make "Silverton a mining town second to none in the state." The rival *San Juan Herald*, on April 27, 1882, was not a step behind. With the coming of the rails, "the difficult problem of our prosperity will then be solved, and we will then have to thank the enterprise and pluck of the much maligned narrow gauge." Having survived a depression, management trials, and disputes with rivals, the D&RG was ready and raring to go.

The first train arrived in July. The *Miner* warned on July 15: "So far, all that can be done by the outside world has been done, for by this medium it has been opened to us—what now remains is for us to do—to commence to make ourselves and make good our statements."

While some did not appreciate the railroad's monopoly, rates, or schedule to their town, the D&RG brought with it a cornucopia of blessings:

lower transportation and freighting costs, quicker access to the outside world, faster year-round service (except during washouts and snow slides), ease of access for investors and everyone else, a lower cost of living, and the most up-to-date transportation available. What more could a district and town want? One of the first investors to arrive in Silverton was Leadville's silver millionaire and Colorado's best-known mining man, Horace Tabor, who purchased some mines, including the very promising Alaska Mine. Where the "big fish go," crowed locals, the "small fish will follow."

For the San Juans, at least in the Silverton area, the future glowed brighter than it ever had. The rest of the region would have to wait a bit, although not a distressingly long time. The D&RG reached Ouray in 1887 and Lake City two years later, having now tapped the San Juans from the south, east, and north.

Otto Mears's Rio Grande Southern Railroad, with generous financial backing from the D&RG, swung around the west side of the mountains, reaching Telluride and Ophir in 1890–91, thus completing the encirclement of the San Juans. From Silverton, three little lines, mostly thanks

Narrow gauge trains could go around sharper curves, go up steeper grades, and be cheaper to build in the mountains. It still took skill and determination to build them, as this trestle on Mears's Rio Grande Southern shows.

The little engines needed plenty of water to navigate over the lines that crisscrossed the San Juans, starting in 1882, when the Denver & Rio Grande reached Silverton. The era of railroad building ended in this region nearly a decade later, when the Rio Grande Southern arrived at Rico and Telluride.

to Mears, rotated out to Red Mountain, Gladstone, Howardsville, and eventually to Animas Forks. Short spur lines also reached out to tap nearby rich mines. The San Juans had come of transportation age.

Nothing brought more joy to the hearts of San Juaners than those little engines' lonesome whistles cascading up and down canyons and circling about mountainsides. Even the puffing smoke brought cheer as the trains rolled past mines and into communities.

All lines adopted the narrow gauge, making it easier to build into the mountains than the four-foot, eight-and-a-half-inch standard gauge. Able to climb steeper grades and to go around sharper curves—and cheaper per mile to build—the narrow gauge offered decided advantages in the mountains. The trade-off came with smaller freight and passenger cars and less powerful engines.

As Silverton's newspapers envisioned, the railroad would bring investors and a host of benefits. Eventually the townspeople understood that tourists would also come, to see the spectacular mountains (and in Ouray and the Animas Valley to enjoy the mineral hot springs that promised rejuvenating miracles) and perhaps sample the wide-open life of the mining towns. They did come, saw, sampled, and traveled home to tell their friends about what was rapidly becoming a legendary America.

As the railroads arrived, getting around by foot and animal also improved over the previous decade. Paths became trails, and trails became roads. Toll roads bedeviled some travelers, Otto Mears being particularly active in this field before he jumped into railroading. But ultimately county roads replaced tollgates, and mules and burros, joined by wagons, hauled their cargoes to isolated camps and mines. Improvements did not stop complaints about road conditions, one of the constants that went on from decade to decade. The roads failed to be maintained to travelers' satisfaction. They seemed too steep, too boggy, too rocky, too narrow, and even too scary. Counties never had enough manpower or money to maintain them as the users wished.

For those mines fortunate enough to be near or on a railroad, the millennium dawned. For those still hours away by narrow trails and unpredictable roads, times grew slightly better than earlier but not as good as those of their more fortunate neighbors. Still, all of the mines benefited

Established by the D&RG in 1880, Durango became southwest Colorado's railroad hub and the smelting center for the mines to the north and west. Hailed as the "magic metropolis," Durango became the largest town in the San Juans, although the only nearby mines were coal.

Otto Mears first built toll roads and then railroads to ease the transportation woes of the San Juans. His home in Silverton still stands. He was involved in everything, from mining to farming, and was active in the negotiations that removed the Utes after the Meeker Massacre, when Nathan Meeker and eleven others were killed in September 1879.

to a degree, and investors, stockholders, and others could definitely arrive with a speed and comfort not seen in Colorado before this generation. Once the ore reached the railroad, it also became easier to transport it to a mill or a smelter.

Now the pace of mining picked up, not leaving agriculture far behind. Mining moved fast, and the transitory life of mines and mining communities left more-sedate easterners and Midwesterners amazed. One notable result of mining's advance was the creation of counties. At one time, in Baker's day, the entire San Juans were divided into Lake and Conejos counties. By 1874, the San Juans had become La Plata, Hinsdale, Rio Grande, and a much-reduced Conejos, with Lake gone. Within eight years, the San Juans had been divided into seven counties, each representing one of the major mining districts. When the town of Creede entered the scene in the 1890s, the last county, Mineral, joined the group. The towns that became county seats gained an unmatchable advantage over their rivals.

Where the railroads could not go, trails to the mines climbed into the mountains.
The Black Bear Road, near Telluride, is an infamous jeep road but offers spectacular
views. Mules could carry up to 250 pounds or so, but little burros only hauled, at
best, 175 to 200 pounds. Legendary in their day, mules and burros both became
folk "heroes" and the subject of innumerable stories.

Becoming a county seat almost guaranteed the permanency that mining could not. Rico built a magnificent county courthouse but lost the cherished designation to Dove Creek after World War II. All the major mining towns gained the honor, and all these communities still stand.

Silverton did not stand alone; it represented only a part of the larger San Juans. Over on the far east side of the San Juan Mountains, Lake City and the farming village of Del Norte promoted themselves as "gateways." The former offered the choice of two high passes to cross Engineer and Cinnamon, both of which entered the region's mountainous center. With a little more riding or walking down the Animas River, Silverton could be reached. Del Norte trumpeted the well-named Stony Pass, which would drop a person into Silverton's neighborhood.

Lake City had been one of Silverton's early rivals. In fact, it had the advantage of being much more open to the outside world, with easier transportation. That advantage could not be discounted. The Lake City district was the first in the San Juans to boom, its mines quickly becoming better known and developed than those in the mountains' interior.

The first boom led to the first bust. In the excited rush of high expectations, claims were staked in valleys and on mountainsides, while booster owners awaited their bonanza either through operation or sales. Alas, for almost all, that never came to pass. "Pockety" ore, small mineral veins, declining ore values, overexpectations, and inexperienced management, along with high developmental costs, put Lake City on the downward circle as early as 1877. On the very southeastern corner of the San Juans, the Summitville district followed a similar course. It too briefly grabbed headlines in the 1870s with its gold (before fading) and within a decade ranked at the bottom of the San Juan mining districts.

Several patterns can be seen emerging here. The San Juans were not settled in one rush; rather, settlement came in a series of smaller rushes to Lake City, Ouray, Telluride, and wherever else even the faintest trace of a mineral outcropping could be found. From 1869 into 1914 ever-optimistic prospectors and miners tramped over these mountains and managed to convince themselves that they, at last, had found the mother lode. Most never came near to finding their fortune.

Every town wanted to have a fancy hotel, where visitors and investors could be comfortably lodged and receive the best culinary meals available. Ouray had the Beaumont, Silverton the Grand Imperial, and Durango the Strater Hotel, shown here, which opened in 1888.

A second trend can be discerned in the early boom and bust of Lake City and Summitville. In any given district or mine, only a finite amount of ore could be found. The deeper the miners blasted, the lower grade ore they dug out and the higher the cost of operations. This had happened throughout western mining and so should have been expected. Optimism, hope, faith, desperation, or inexperience led people to believe somehow that their mine would be different. The lessons of mining history eventually caught up with them all.

Another tendency, discussed more in chapter two, was the urbanization of mining. The more-prosperous towns with their greater populations, larger, more-varied business and entertainment districts, more-substantial buildings, and quite often county courthouses came to dominate the local scene. Around them would gather the far more-numerous little camps. Like a mother bear watching her cubs, the towns guarded against interlopers trying to steal business from their hinterland. Ouray versus Silverton, Telluride versus Rico—they fought with urban rivalries and jealousies that would have done more-established eastern towns proud.

The railroad brought boom to already-promising districts. Ouray always had promise, but it faced a problem. With the Ute reservation only two miles away, all goods into the district had to come through Ute land.

No San Juan mine became more famous than Ouray's Camp Bird. It made Thomas Walsh the district's first millionaire and produced over $27 million (mostly gold) from 1896–1916, when gold was $20 and change per ounce. The general manager's home displays the fame and wealth of the mine.

Until 1881, that carried with it risks, but then, with the Utes gone, the route opened, and farmers and ranchers swarmed into the fertile Uncompahgre Valley just to the north. This proved even better than Silverton's situation, with the Animas Valley to the south, where two mountain passes challenged freighters carrying in goods (until the railroad arrived). Produce and animals could reach Ouray via a gentle river valley.

Mining had reached the San Juans, and already the impact spread like a rock hitting a pond. Improved transportation arrived, agriculture took root, tourists gathered, and urbanization sprang up in some highly unlikely places as well as predictable ones. Mineral Point, in a high, isolated little mountain valley, illustrated the former, and Rico, along the beautiful Dolores River Valley, the latter.

Prospectors may have reached Ouray at about the time of the Baker fiasco, but they did not stay either. Back came others in the 1870s, yet still the district struggled, its mines neither as rich nor attracting as much attention as those of its neighbors. Then in the 1890s, one of the great mines in

American history was discovered and developed just southwest of town, the Camp Bird. For a decade, it maintained high gold production, represented the best of current mining methods and equipment, attracted visitors throughout the world, and made its original owner, Thomas Walsh, the only San Juan man to reach that goal of so many, millionaire status.

A stone's throw north of Ouray, other mines opened, and at the turn of the century the district enjoyed long-awaited prosperity. Situated at the very north edge of the San Juans, Ouray represented one apex of the mining heart of the San Juans. A triangle with Ouray, Telluride, and Silverton as its points defines the grouping of the richest and most famous of the San Juan mines. All of these properties came into major production with gold in the 1890s, closely paralleling the Camp Bird.

Telluride was the most isolated of all the districts in the entire region. Separated by passes and mountains from all its neighbors, it languished until the coming of the Rio Grande Southern. Prospectors had arrived in the 1870s; dismally slow growth followed. Spring after spring encouraging reports appeared, only to be dashed in the shadow of isolation, altitude, and all the other problems that faced each district in its youth.

The railroad made all the difference, and the long wait for boom proved profitable beyond even the dreams of some of the district's boosters. Its mines equaled or surpassed the nearby Camp Bird. The Tomboy, Smuggler-Union, and Liberty Bell, with their lesser neighbors, brought Telluride into its greatest days in the 1890s and the first decade of the new century. It became the "belle" of the district. The wait proved worth the time and effort.

Silverton finally enjoyed a long-awaited major boom when the Silver Lake and Gold King mines, among others, came into their own. For each of these prosperous and well-known districts, a half dozen or so flourished briefly, then faded. Rico started early and had a few years of good times but by the 1890s had seen better days. Creede, where "it's day all day in the daytime, and there is no night in Creede," had its moments. Its mines prospered for a few years in the 1890s, and then the hard times came, through no fault of its own. Production continued despite setbacks, and eventually it became the third major silver producer of the San Juans.

The San Juans pioneered in the use of trams to overcome elevation and isolation.
The buckets could carry ore, supplies, coal, and even brave people up and down
the mountainsides. Ouray newspaper editor Dave Day realized the significance
of trams: "The invention revolutionizes mining in this section."

Animas Forks, Howardsville, Rose's Cabin, Red Mountain, Parrott City, Ames, Mineral Point, and other towns all had their brief flurries of excitement. Each faced problems of isolation, winter weather, pockets of rich ore declining to low grade, and, after the flush of prosperity passed, difficulties in attracting investors. By the start of World War I, all had seen better days, and a very few, like Eureka, still held out promise, primarily because of new milling methods that allowed base metals to be profitably mined.

Yet the excitement had not yet ended. In 1914, a new discovery in Cave Basin, on the border of La Plata and Hinsdale counties, lured in a share of rushers. Some came in cars: a new age had dawned. Neighboring Durango and Bayfield both claimed to be the gateway this time. As the crow flies, Cave Basin was not that far away from La Plata Canyon, where, back in the early 1870s, John Moss had promoted his discoveries, some of the first in the region. Men came by horseback and foot then, and the nearest town of any size was Santa Fe.

An architect would probably shudder at this strange Rube Goldberg–like creation. It did, however, allow the miners to go from the mine to the bunkhouse with stops in between without having to face the blasts of a San Juan winter high in Picayune Gulch.

Into these beehive-shaped coke ovens went bituminous coal. Out came coke after heating had driven off the "volatile constituents." Coke burned hotter and proved excellent for smelting ore. This bank of ovens is near Redstone; none in the San Juans survive. The largest group were in Durango, next to the smelter.

The end results proved familiar. Forecasts of rich strikes, hundreds if not thousands rushing into the basin, and great production missed the mark completely. Many claims and small production seemed familiar, as did the gentle quietness that settled over the district within a year. By that time, the world struggled at war, and many Americans wondered if their country might join the carnage that a twentieth-century war produced.

This sketch of the leaps and jerks of San Juan mining development falls short of telling the whole story. It provides a framework whose substance came from what else happened. Obviously gold and silver production caught most people's attention. With San Miguel and Ouray counties leading the way, gold production topped $126 million, and the Telluride district produced over 40 percent of that total. Silver production topped $99 million, with Ouray and San Miguel counties the main producers.

Less glamorous and catching few headlines but important nevertheless were the base metals, which added to the wealth being mined out of the San Juans. Lead contributed $34 million, copper $10 million, and zinc $3 million, with San Juan County leading the way in all three. Coal also contributed to the mineral treasure, with La Plata County producing over four million tons of it during these years. While far below the production in

The ubiquitous boardinghouse was found throughout the San Juans. This one served miners in Picayune Gulch, southwest of Animas Forks. Mining engineer Eben Olcott described one at the North Star as about twenty by twenty feet, with twenty-seven men crowded into it, "nearly all of whom smoke." Add to this the drying of wet clothes and "the aroma is delicious as you can imagine."

Colorado's major coalfields, these coal mines satisfied regional needs. At the moment it offered only a fascinating sidelight, but on the western fringe of San Miguel County, pitchblende and carnotite, from which uranium could be refined, were being mined. Medical and scientific research provided the prime markets.

A trend obvious throughout these decades was the quick dominance of corporation mining. Small mine owners would be around for the entire period, but large companies soon gobbled up many of the best small claims and mines and consolidated them into the major mines. This was a benefit in the sense that the large companies had the finances, management, and generally the skill to develop the ore bodies for a longer period. They also could afford the latest equipment and use innovative mining methods. These mines can be credited with by far the largest percentage of San Juan production. In the laborers' view, however, they faced corporation dominance, a tendency seen throughout American industry during these years.

THE ARRIVAL OF
THE MINERS

Industrialization had arrived in the San Juans with all its benefits and drawbacks. Wage work would be measured by time and controlled by bosses calling into question the miners' professionalism and freedom. That planted the seed for trouble over wages, working conditions, and union recognition. Also, when one of these mines shut down, the impact throughout the district and nearby communities could be devastating.

To mine all this ore took skill, hard work, determination, finances, and reduction plants to separate waste from and refine valuable ores. Initially, almost all of the mining process was done by hand or simple methods. Then innovations and machines helped the miners and mill men along. Yet much had not changed. By 1914, a miner of 1870 would still have recognized the dangerous, strenuous work that it took to mine ore from underground and move it to the surface. Nor would he have thought the pay had improved all that much either.

Miners, muckers, trammers, station tenders, machine men, powder monkeys, mill men, shift bosses, timbermen, superintendents, common laborers, blacksmiths, host engineers, nippers—they had many names, depending on what they did under- or aboveground. The pay for most of them did not compensate for the dangers involved. A skilled miner might earn $2.50 to $3.50 a day, depending on the year, muckers (who shoveled the ore into the mine cars) and laborers a little less, and machine men (power drills) $3.50 or so. More-skilled workers, such as blacksmiths, pump men, and engineers, earned $4.00 to $4.50 per day. If the men lived in the company boardinghouse, a dollar per day was deducted for room and board. By 1900 workers underground generally worked an eight-hour day and those aboveground a nine- or ten-hour shift. These wages varied over the years but did not represent near the contribution these men made to the dividends that traveled back to eastern or foreign investors.

Coal mining, with its gas and unstable rock, remained far more dangerous than hard rock mining. For this, coal miners, who worked in teams of two, earned even less. They were paid by the ton mined, depending on the time, 35 to 60 cents. Recent immigrants from eastern European countries or Hispanics were much more likely to be found mining coal than northern Europeans. Americans and northern Europeans dominated the hard rock industry, although others had made inroads by the century's turn.

Initially miners drilled by hand, either individually or as a double-jack team, into the hard granite rock to bore the holes for a round of blasting. Then after the air cleared, muckers would muck the ore into ore cars and trammers would take it to the surface. Until the introduction of more powerful and dangerous dynamite, black powder served as the explosive. Dynamite, in the hands of a skilled miner, could break more rock, moving production along.

"Whither is fled the visionary gleam? Where is it now, the glory and the dream?" asked the English poet William Wordsworth. Men and ore once came out of this portal of the Camp Bird Mine. Now they are gone, and it awaits the ravages of time.

The Arrival of
the Miners

The introduction of power drills in the 1880s allowed the miners to drill more holes in less time with an ease unimaginable in earlier days. But the miners were not happy: they had a longtime prejudice against new machines that might threaten their jobs. Machine drilling negated their hand skills and took away some of the professionalism of their work. Almost anyone could be trained to operate a drill in a relatively short time. Furthermore, those early drills ground rapier-sharp dust into the air, unloosing a deadly killer, silicosis, or, as they called it, "miners' consumption." That danger was finally reduced by hollowing out the center of the drill and flushing water through it into the hole being bored. Eventually the miners came to appreciate the laborsaving and time-saving drills, and, particularly in the larger mines, use of these drills became a way of life fairly quickly.

The major companies also introduced bathing and drying rooms at the mine's portal to help their miners avoid colds and dreaded pneumonia and to stop "high grading," or stealing ore. Most companies also hired a company doctor who was available on-site or in a nearby town. Be that as it may, miners still risked their lives every time they entered a mine. Cave-ins, falling rock, premature blasts, missed holes, breaking of a hoist cable, falling down shafts, their own carelessness, and electrocution (coming into contact with a live wire) caused an alarming toll of injuries and death.

Electricity proved a major blessing and a small curse, particularly those bare, live wires in wet mines. That did not deter the mining companies in the San Juans from pioneering in the use of alternating current for industrial purposes. Why? The high cost of buying and hauling coal and wood to mountainous, isolated mines cut into profits and could even prevent their profitable operation. Lucien Nunn, manager of the Gold King Mine, southwest of Telluride, faced just that problem. He turned to that new development, electricity, and the Westinghouse Electric Company. The result was the construction of a power plant at Ames, on the south fork of the San Miguel River. In the spring of 1891, the plant transmitted the first alternating current over a long distance. A new age had been born.

Innumerable benefits for mining arrived with electricity. From lighting to operation of the hoist lifting the cage up and down the shaft to power for a host of machines, this wonder changed the industry. Boardinghouses could be heated and lighted by electricity, improving the miners' leisure hours. Even more benefits came to the nearby communities.

Electricity also began to power the trams, which proved pivotal in helping overcome the distance, bad weather, elevation, and isolation problems that haunted the San Juans. Although not developed in the San Juans, these systems of buckets running on cables supported by towers (think modern ski lifts) ran from mill or railroad siding to the mines far

Mining companies pioneered in the use of electricity as well as trams in the San Juans. The Ames Power Plant, south of Telluride, has been operating since 1891. Water from Trout Lake turns an undershoot waterwheel to generate electricity. Telluride folk used to come out to see it start, as smoke shot out and sparks flew, rivaling a fireworks fanfare.

above. Supplies could be taken up and injured miners down, and game miners would ride them both ways. Before the century turned, some of these trams stretched several miles around and up mountainsides. Snow slides might create havoc by knocking out towers, but they were repaired and operation resumed.

Electricity also improved life in the mills and smelters. Raw ore taken from the earth must be worked to separate value from waste. Like most mining districts, the San Juans went through a trial-and-error period before what methods worked best with local ore were discovered. By 1900, a variety of processes could be used in smelters, depending on the ore complexity.

For most mining companies, it proved unprofitable to build their own mill or smelter at the mine, and so mill owners purchased ore or contracted to refine it. A variation had concentrating mills separating much of the

Lucien Nunn, managing the Gold King Mine, above Ophir, found his fuel expenses undermining profitable operation. He turned to George Westinghouse and alternating current, and success followed. Mining took on a new dimension with this, the first AC commercial venture.

Tram cables crisscrossed the San Juan skyline like spiderwebs. Some were short; others ran for several miles. Aerial tramways stretched to mines throughout the district, and "tramway men," including gripmen, bucketmen, brakemen, oilers, and linemen, kept them operating.

The Solid Democrat Mill served the mines in Placer Gulch and has been stabilized to preserve a part of the San Juans' fleeting past.

gangue (waste rock) and then shipping the remaining higher-grade ore by rail to a large smelter. It also was easier to ship ore downhill than to haul fuel, equipment, and needed production materials uphill.

Thus regional smelters developed. For the San Juans, this meant Durango, the "smelter city," where coal was mined nearby, transportation proved better, plenty of water was available, and the climate was usually milder. The region's largest community, it provided a host of conveniences that could not be found elsewhere, another benefit for management and workers.

Another sign of the changing times was that the San Juans had become part of the larger world of mining conditions. This came drastically to the forefront with the declining price of silver. With fewer countries using silver coinage (its price floated on the world market, making financial stability difficult) and with industrial use and jewelry and plate sales not significantly increasing, the price of silver dropped steadily from the 1870s into the 1890s. Colorado, San Juan miners, and silver miners everywhere could do nothing about it, although it had a severe impact on their operations and profits. Eventually the "silver issue" became an American political issue.

The federal government refused to subsidize the silver-mining industry with a guaranteed price despite western demands, although it did buy silver for coinage. This finally resulted in the famous "battle of the standards" (gold versus silver) in the 1896 presidential election. Silver lost. Gloom and despair settled over the mountains, made worse by the worldwide economic crash and depression of 1893, which stretched into the following years. Fortunately the San Juans could shift to gold as the primary precious metal mined. Nonetheless, something had been lost—the spirit, the dash, the confidence that had marked those earlier decades. In mining terms, the San Juans were getting along in years.

Trains, drills, trams, electricity, corporation control, world issues—all changed life in the San Juan mining districts. By the 1890s, the days of the "jackass" prospector were gone, and it was hello to company dominance and absentee ownership. No longer with much reality of success could a miner turned prospector "tramp down the hill" and discover his own mine.

Inside the Solid Democrat, batteries of stamps crushed the crude ore from the mine into finer particles so that mercury could be introduced to separate the gold from the gangue, or waste rock. Mark Twain once worked in a mill, an experience he did not relish. "One of us stood by the battery all day long, breaking up masses of silver-bearing rocks and shoveling it into the battery."

Occasionally mills were built somewhere else and moved, as in the case of the Bagley Mill. Numbered beams guided the reconstruction. The cyanide vat indicates a turn-of-the-century improvement over older processes. Cyanide provided an easy and cheap way to separate gold from other materials.

Tram buckets carried ore from mine to mill, simplifying mining and limiting costly freighting by wagon or mule. From the 1870s to the 1920s, tramways were developed and improved on, one of the innovations that transformed western mining. Ski lifts evolved from the tram idea.

New machines, new methods, industrialization, and corporations took some of the skill, opportunity, and professionalism out of the miner's life.

Modernization of mining did not simply evolve in the mining West. It happened all over the United States. The predictable came to pass—the formation of unions to give the worker more voice and power. For the miner, this meant the Western Federation of Miners, organized in 1893. Local unions had already started in the San Juans but lacked the clout to win many victories. Joined with miners throughout the West, the WFM gained the power to challenge management. The predictable again ensued. In 1894, Colorado entered a two-decade struggle between owners and labor that started in the hard rock district of Cripple Creek and ended with the coal miners at Ludlow in April 1914.

The issues seemed simple to the San Juan miners—wages, safety and health laws, hours, recognition of the union. Management, however, balked. The two sides warily circled each other while tensions and bitterness mounted. Paralleling what had transpired elsewhere, some strikes initially flared, including a Durango smelter strike. Then in 1903–4, a major strike hit the industry from Cripple Creek to Telluride. Intimidation, violence, violation of civil rights, huge local and state expenses, and a poor image for Colorado followed. When the smoke cleared, management had won. In the San Juans, the union cause was dead for decades. The action then shifted to the coalfields far beyond the San Juans. Although the union may have lost this critical round, its heritage lived on, including two hospitals, in Telluride and Silverton, built with members' money.

Miners have always labored in a dangerous occupation. Alfred King, himself blinded by a mining accident, wrote that miners faced "dangers more grim than the cannon's mouth." Fortunate was the mining town that had a hospital, such as Telluride's, built in 1893. Telluride actually had two hospitals for a brief time. The Western Federation of Miners built one in 1902, which closed during the 1903–4 strike.

Altogether, company dominance, inventions, innovations, and labor disputes amounted to the end of the era, the era of the opening of the West. Gone was the day of the prospector, the town organizer, the railroad builder, the pioneer rancher—the West that artist Charles Russell so loved. "The West is dead, my friend," he wrote in 1917.

The coming of the automobile, the "aeroplane," the motion picture, electric appliances, the "silver issue," labor disputes, industrialization, and World War I marked the close of the epic. The San Juans were settled and already in some places abandoned, particularly those small camps whose mines had declined and departed. Mining had passed its peak, and so had the population of most mining towns. Already a yearning for the "old days" surfaced.

Despite these yearnings, times were changing. A popular song of a few years back observed, "Those were the days, my friend, we thought they'd never end." The San Juaners should have seen it coming, like a warm summer day slipping into a chilly autumn evening. Nor would there be the dawning of a fresh spring to follow a bitter, snowbound San Juan winter. Mining would continue on and does, into the twenty-first century, in a small way. That hope for a better tomorrow, which characterizes so much that happened since 1869 in the San Juans, lingers on. Who can say that someday over the next mountain there won't be a rich strike?

For the miner in the twenty-first century, the world has changed. No longer is he the herald of Manifest Destiny, the maker of a better America. Might he, or now she, still return to the San Juans for another search for the mother lode? Yet the odds are less than even on finding a rich lode. If perchance such a lode was found, financial costs, the lack of a supportive mining environment, volatile world metal prices, little mining infrastructure, and environmental concerns and laws would make it a new era for the miner, unlike any his or her pioneer ancestors encountered. So those freewheeling optimistic days have become a thing of the past, a past that will not rise up like the phoenix to start anew.

How does one measure this era? In the opera *The Ballad of Baby Doe*, Horace Tabor, an old man seemingly defeated by life, poses that question:

> *How can a man measure himself?*
> *The land was growing and I grew with it.*
> *In my brain rose buildings yearning towards the sky,*
> *And my guts sank deep in the plunging mineshafts*
> *My feet kicked up gold dust wherever I danced*
> *And whenever I shouted my name*
> *I heard a silver echo roar in the wind.*

The old San Juaner, who had come in the 1870s and seen it all, could

just as easily have asked the same question as a world war started to over-run the second decade of the twentieth century. Already much of his youthful days whispered merely as an echo in the wind. Now sites and relics of a bygone era seemed only strange and fascinating, somewhat leg-endary too, to the 1914 modern ragtime youth with their phonographs, cars, and airplanes. The pace had been fast and hectic and seemed to be picking up speed.

The results were mixed and the cost high of those earlier mining activities. The land was scarred, and so were individual lives. The moun-tains had never really been tamed, but plenty of evidence existed that puny man had tried his best.

Poet Alfred King, blinded in a San Juan mining accident, captured the temper of the onrushing silence that appeared even as the tempo of mining hastened by about the turn of the twentieth century. In his poem "The Ruined Cabin," King pictured the dreams now turned to despair as he opened his elegy:

Cinnamon Pass connects Lake City and Silverton and
along it rest the remains of mining days including this dam.

The Arrival of
the Miners

There's a pathos in the solemn desolation
Of the mountain cabin sinking in decay,
With its threshold overgrown with vegetation,
With its door unhinged and mouldering away.

Man had not done this. Broken dreams and time, King concluded, "with rust and ruin fraught" left the cabin in decay and "all are subject to the same disintegration."

What had these several generations of Coloradans and outsiders accomplished? They had opened the land, developed its resources, and promoted its wonders far beyond the craggy mountains, deep canyons, and river-carved valleys that they called home. The agricultural, tourist, transportation, urban, and cultural foundations they intentionally, or not, established remained. These San Juaners had produced wealth, much of which migrated into pocketbooks, wallets, and banks in faraway places that knew the San Juans only in passing. Some of their communities would survive, particularly those that had been fortunate enough to be named the county seat.

These folks and their endeavors produced the "lasting heritage" part of the larger story of Colorado and the American West. They had not been intentionally caught up in something larger than themselves; it just happened as part of life. In the end, little glory or fame came their way. There was just a lot of backbreaking hard work, skimpy rewards, moments of laughter and tears and of joys and sorrows, and a certain satisfaction in realizing they were part of something greater than themselves in the story of the San Juans, Colorado, and the Rocky Mountain region.

Maybe their children remained or came back to see where their parents had lived. They remembered; they understood. For their grandchildren and great-grandchildren much has been forgotten and, perhaps, the rest little appreciated. The Tomboy Mine or a Saturday night's dance at Rose's Cabin happened a long time ago in a far different epoch, yet much can still be understood and savored by taking the time to look and ponder. It is the story that the San Juans can still tell about those who came before.

THE ARRIVAL OF
THE MINERS

Perched some 2,400 feet above Cunningham Gulch, the Old One Hundred boarding- house and tram terminus graphically illustrate the trials and tribulations of San Juan mining. For the operation of mines so high up, boardinghouses proved essential, and the miners paid $1 per day in the nineteenth century to stay in them. The cook was one of the most important people around!

*At one time, lumbermen built their mills and cut their
timber, and then frame buildings appeared, along
with wooden shingles on the roof. Mining beckoned
others to come and make a living aboveground.*

SAN JUAN URBANIZATION

WITH DREAMS OF SILVER RICHES, THAT PENULTIMATE MINER/REPORTER Mark Twain ventured to make his fortune in Nevada's early 1860s mining boom. Alas, he failed and journeyed on to the exuberant "flush times" in Virginia City, which basked in the midst of its first Comstock bonanza. Here Twain started his writing career, which eventually led him to become one of America's most popular authors. Recounting those days with a touch of sentimental nostalgia, he nonetheless captured that bygone era:

> The city of Virginia roosted royally midway up the steep side of Mount Davidson . . . and in the clear Nevada atmosphere was visible from a distance of fifty miles! It claimed a population of fifteen thousand to eighteen thousand, and all day long half of this little army swarmed the streets like bees and the other half swarmed among the drifts and tunnels of the "Comstock."

> To show what a wild spirit possessed the mining brain of the community, I will remark that "claims" were actually "located" in excavations for cellars, where the pick had exposed what seemed to be quartz veins.

> Money was wonderfully plenty. The trouble was, not how to get it—but how to spend it, how to lavish it, get rid of it, squander it.

With a fine touch, the onetime steamboat pilot and Confederate soldier grasped the spirit, the flare, the excitement of the nineteenth-century mining West. San Juan communities never reached the status of their

The miner far up in the San Juans had no time for planting and harvesting a crop, nor would the elevation permit it. Neither would he find much entertainment or businesses near his cabin. Down in the valleys, they awaited him.

Nevada contemporary. That didn't mean, however, that they didn't try. Nor did they lack the flavor of the times, just the great wealth that Twain described. Nor did Twain arrive to be their Homer.

The mining West was never a frontier in the true definition of the word. It might have been isolated, a far distance from the nearest settlement, have had a tenuous transportation system, and have faced hostile tribes who found their land being overrun, but first and foremost, urbanization dominated it. When hundreds, occasionally thousands of people arrived in a few weeks and established settlements, developed roads, and opened mines, any thought of an isolated, thinly settled frontier vanished. It had been true in 1849, in 1859, and absolutely in the 1870s, when the San Juans finally opened.

Prospectors and miners had little time or inclination to plant crops or develop the rudiments of civilization beyond their claim or mine. Hence others came to "mine the miners," who in theory, at least, pocketed gold or silver to pay for needed services, entertainment, and goods. Small

Around the larger mines, little settlements often took root. The Ute-Ulay Mine, west of Lake City, proved to be one of the more productive mines in this district. It especially attracted attention when an assay ran 650 ounces of silver to the ton.

Water power made milling much cheaper, if it could possibly be harnessed.
The Ute-Ulay owners constructed a dam to yoke nature's bounty on
Henson Creek. Electricity, too, was generated on some rivers.

mining camps grew high on mountain slopes and snuggled in river valleys and along isolated canyon bottoms. With luck, these camps evolved
into a larger mining town that came to dominate the camps within its
economic sphere. Most did not grow beyond camp status and shriveled
as their nearby mines declined. Some camps were gone in a year or two.
Others lasted a decade or so before becoming a relic of yesterday and a
sign of long-departed expectations.

All mining camps chronicled the expectations and aspirations of a
generation of hopeful Americans who left behind a beguiling heritage for
those who wander about the San Juans today. Without these camps and
towns, San Juan mining could not have established and maintained itself.
They provided both the substance and the stability that undergirded mining in the forty years of San Juan fame and fortune.

No permanent settlement came with the Spanish incursions into these
mountains. The first briefly took root with the Baker party in Animas City,
far down the Animas River south from the mountains. It lasted no longer
than the aborted rush of 1861. By the time prospectors returned, little
remained of it except a few scattered timbers to show pioneers had resided
there, their aspirations long since gone in the morning light.

The lure of gold never died, despite the failure of the initial rush.
Back came the hopeful in 1869—and again in 1870. They prospected,

staked claims, knew they had found a "mine," and retreated before winter snows cut them off from "civilization." Back the next spring came the optimistic, up the valleys into the mountains. It soon became obvious that at least some mines held a promising future that could be developed best by year-round operation. With the nearest settlements several strenuous days' travel away across the San Juans in the San Luis Valley—or weeks away in New Mexico Territory—these San Juaners needed a nearby permanent base. No option remained; settlement had to come to the San Juans.

It came in the mountains and south along the Animas River. Each little settlement envisioned itself as a soon-to-be "metropolis" of the San Juans, and some came close to attaining that goal. By the mid-1870s, Lake City, on the eastern fringe of the San Juans, had emerged as the gateway, joined farther south by the farming-ranching village of Del Norte. In the heart of the mountains, Silverton grew, where the miners of 1861 had failed to find enough gold to tempt them to stay. On the north side of the San Juans, Ouray nestled in a beautiful valley along the Uncompahgre River, and on the west side, later in the decade, Rico, Ames, Ophir, and Columbia came into existence.

Almost all of these eventually grew from camps into towns. The towns had a more substantial population and a greater business district, construction beyond log and frame buildings, and larger and more prosperous mines nearby (which in itself promised a longevity that their smaller neighbors could only envy). They became the county seat with all that represented and exhibited a demeanor that could not be found in the more numerous camps. Each of these towns had smaller camps in its economic orbit, and woe unto a rival who tried to "steal" one by dominating its trade and business.

Scattered about to serve nearby mines were a host of camps with a variety of names and futures. Gladstone, named after the English prime minister, lay up Cement Creek by Silverton. Howardsville, north of Silverton, had once been its rival but lost out even though Howardsville was at the mouth of Cunningham Gulch, one of the main routes into the San Juans. Nearby Neigoldstown and Bullion City lasted only a couple of seasons. Traveling north up the Animas River, a traveler reached Eureka and, beyond that, Animas Forks. Mineral Point, which claimed to be the "highest miners' camp in the country," struggled for existence even farther up the mountains. Originally called Mineral City, the town had been named by boomers, who loved to attach the title "city" to their little communities: "city" conjectured future hopes and maybe fooled a potential investor or two, who imagined more than actually existed. Parrott City on the southwestern fringe of La Plata Mountains did the same thing.

*No camp was more isolated than Carson, which had two sections straddling
the Continental Divide. The* Lake City Times *(June 13, 1895) claimed
Carson "is beginning to wake up" after being "asleep for nearly three years."
It never got beyond a big yawn and soon went back to sleep.*

Over by Lake City, on two routes into the heart of the mountains, popped up an array of little camps. Along the trail that crossed Engineer Pass were Henson, Capitol City, and Rose's Cabin, while Sherman, White Cross, Tellurium, and Argentum struggled for existence near the Cinnamon Pass route. Some of them never emerged beyond the "several cabin" stage and their founders' overly optimistic wishes.

Near Telluride, Rock Point soon disappeared, but Ophir lasted. San Miguel City, meanwhile, merged with neighboring Columbia to become Telluride. In the far southeastern corner of the San Juan district, Summitville had its moment of fame and prosperity. The miners needed food, and, to answer that need, farmers and ranchers settled south in the Animas Valley, where the lower elevation, longer growing season, and milder climate allowed them to flourish. Animas City, same name but a different location than the 1861 failure, survived, while several rivals, such as Elbert, faded from memory. The Uncompahgre Valley opened too, and so did agricultural land west of Telluride. The farmer had come to stay.

There were and would be other towns as the San Juan mining district ebbed and flowed over the next thirty years. Frank Fossett, in his *Colorado* (1880 edition), summarized Ouray's and Silverton's attractions and attributes. Every neighboring rival aspired to and often claimed the same advantages. Besides their numerous and "extremely rich" nearby mineral veins and mines, towns professed other blessings, including being the county seat. Silverton "is a growing and prosperous mining town," wrote Fossett, and "few towns in the world" could match Ouray's beautiful location and "grand and majestic scenery." It also had "health-giving" mineral waters, those medical elixirs of the nineteenth century. With that beautiful scenery, those hot springs, and its budding mining history came the seeds of future tourism, which developed remarkably quickly in the 1880s.

Each community provided a microcosm of the Victorian society that these Coloradans had left behind in their old homes. And they had come from everywhere to try their luck in this new and promising mining district. Who were they? The census of 1880, for example, disclosed that

When Otto Mears's Rio Grande Southern Railroad finally reached Telluride in 1891, that district ultimately boomed to become the San Juans' richest. Wrote a correspondent to the Engineering and Mining Journal *(January 21, 1892), this "insures a large and increasing output from Telluride."*

native-born Americans predominated, especially with the increasing percentage of Colorado-born children. The East and Midwest contributed the next-highest percentages. The largest group of foreigners came from Britain, followed by Germany.

The San Juaners were young, averaging in their early thirties, literate (or so they said), and often single. About a quarter of them were or had been married, but many did not bring their families into this new mining region. Over half of the men listed their occupation as miners, and native-born Americans dominated in what might be described as white-collar occupations. Foreigners, on the other hand, often found themselves in jobs that generally required a great deal of physical stamina. This picture did not particularly differ from that of other contemporary mining regions and communities.

Passengers wishing to wet their whistle in Telluride had only to walk down Pacific Avenue from the depot. Walking a little farther, they reached the Senate, part of Telluride's red-light district. Gambling, prostitution, drinking, dancing—a host of entertainments were offered there. "All sorts of doings around the tenderloin district," reported the San Miguel Examiner.

Boardwalks and false-fronted buildings made up Lake City's business center. Businessmen and businesswomen were the heart and soul of a mining camp or town. They invested more and risked more on the future than most of their neighbors.

No better way to help re-create the life left behind than to have an opera house grace the main street, although opera was seldom performed. Ouray's Wright Opera House has a cast-iron front, the likes of which could be ordered in various styles.

In their communities, they struggled to re-create what they remembered or desired from their old homes. The physical setting might be very different, but that made little difference. The familiar created a sense of security, permanence, and stability. It might also entice others to come and settle or invest money. Either one was a definite plus in the "grow or die" world of the late nineteenth century.

If someone from modern times could have visited these mining towns, much that bedrocked urbanization would have quickly become apparent. Walking down the main street of a mining town would have given the visitor a glimpse of familiar businesses. For example, in 1884, Telluride offered customers a choice of grocery stores; miners' supply businesses; drug-, jewelry, hardware, dry goods, and furniture stores; a bank; restaurants; and rooming and lodging houses. There were also a barbershop, livery stables, lumberyards, a theater, and a variety of saloons. Silverton, four years later, offered all that plus a hotel, fresh fruit stand, bakery, and boot and shoe store. Lake City had several other types of business, including two bookstores, a cigar store, and a brewery.

Mining towns also had a variety of fraternal lodges, some with impressive buildings. The high tide of lodges came in the nineteenth century. In the transitory life of mining, they provided a particularly welcome door into the community, a sense of belonging and fellowship, which often included insurance and social outlets. An opera house, even if an opera performance proved as rare as a robin in winter, glistened as the crown jewel in many a town's aspirations.

The mining camps could not offer that variety. In 1880, Capitol City contained a hotel, a general merchandise store, and three saloons. In 1882, Animas Forks had a general store, restaurant, hotel, and livery stable. Red Mountain, part of the new district opening in the 1880s between Silverton and Ouray, offered a saloon, butcher, furniture store, drugstore, hotel, livery stable, boardinghouse, and grocery in 1883.

Beyond the main street, the visitor could have seen another difference between mining towns and mining camps. Mining towns had large frame homes, often modeled after the latest Victorian architectural styles, moderate-size frame dwellings, and, of course, a smattering of log cabins.

Miners near the mines lived in boardinghouses, such as the Kohler Boarding House, which unfortunately was destroyed soon after this photograph was taken.

Probably one of the most-photographed buildings in the mining
San Juans, this Victorian home stands in Animas Forks, an example
of trying to reproduce the "old home." Most small mining camps
had nothing like this structure, but the larger towns did.

A mining camp might have one or two examples of such fancier homes. Animas Forks had a large frame one, for instance, but most of the homes were either log cabins or small frame structures. Expectations ran high in all communities, but reality limited development.

Another factor separated towns from camps—a local newspaper. In the dog-eat-dog world of nineteenth-century personal journalism, it was extremely important that a community have a voice. The newspaper promoted local and nearby attractions and development, defended the home-town against "jealous" rivals, served as the community gadfly, encouraged investors and others to come, and nourished "culture" and a host of other refinements. Consequently newspaper wars flared with regularity, if only briefly until something new seized the editors' attention. The mining West believed wholeheartedly in the blessings that newspapers brought. Usually a weekly surfaced. A daily edition indicated the bounties of prosperity and growth or possibly overexpectations.

San Juan towns all had their press champions riding to defend and illuminate. Indeed, competition remained the spice of life in most of these communities. Creede, an 1890s addition to the district, jumped into the fray with four newspapers, then reality stepped in and, by 1900, only two remained. Lake City did likewise, having during its 1870s boom days at one time three newspapers, finally settling down to two and then just one. Telluride, showing its size and importance, offered local folks at least six newspaper choices during the first decade of its existence. The life span of these papers could be short as editors and press moved on to a more promising site. Rico, for instance, during the first twenty years of its life had ten different newspapers, only one lasting as long as six years.

Mining camps struggled to secure similar spokesmen. Red Mountain, during its two decades of existence, had an amazing total of seven news-papers, five of which lasted barely a year, and one published only seven months before giving up the ghost. Since Red Mountain's peak summer population seldom topped a couple of hundred and often slipped to less than a hundred during the winter, such efforts illustrated hope over reality. The only thing that kept the newspapers going most of the time was the publication of patented claim notices, as required by federal mining law. Ophir's one newspaper, in contrast, lasted a decade, and Bachelor, Creede's neighbor, had three during its existence, but they never provided continuous coverage. Most mining camps had none, and their prospects suffered accordingly.

If a camp or town hoped to have an air of permanence, a church or several churches provided an excellent reminder of home and a stable, set-tled community. This did not mean that one had to attend. Just the build-ing, with a steeple and bell, gave the right impression. With Sunday being

Lake City's Presbyterian Church and manse resulted from the work of George Darley, one of the most successful of San Juan ministers. Darley wrote that in "no region" can you find men "so indifferent to religious influence as in a new mining camp." He "suffered and suffered again" to advance his faith, to promote temperance, and to keep Christians from "going straight to hell."

a wide-open business day, the minister or priest faced the daunting task of gathering the flock, usually women and their children, while their menfolk attended to business. Single miners were less apt to appear, what with other attractions beckoning. Women, however, found the church a great outlet for reform movements (antigambling and prohibition, for instance) and a place to exercise leadership while the men worked.

Despite long hours spent trying to make a living in mining communities, people found time for recreation. The town baseball team (some camps had them too) defended local honor and strove to win its supporters' bets, confidently placed on the boys to bring home a win, as might the town's fastest runner against a rival. Single and double drilling contests allowed miners to display their skills long after they no longer needed them in the mines. Races between competing fire companies generated excitement and displayed needed expertise. The Christmas season and

July 4 were the big holidays, although Valentine's Day and Thanksgiving also provided relaxation. Dances were always popular, as were picnics in the summer.

Women, because of their "scarcity," found that the mining communities were much more liberal in their attitude to what feminine roles might be. Obviously wife and mother predominated, but women found other avenues open to them. They dominated the teaching, domestic, and seamstress occupations. Women came close to controlling the rooming and boardinghouse trade and occasionally operated hotels. To a lesser degree, they ran other businesses and might even be found in such male-dominated professions as physician and newspaper editor. They did not have to put up with an abusive husband or a failed marriage. Little social stigma lay in divorce, and plenty more congenial future spouses lived in and around town. When the time came, women also found strong support for women's suffrage in the mining regions. Women dominated the

Opened in 1881, this Congregational church still serves Silverton. Preaching in Silverton in 1878, the Reverend Joseph Pickett held a meeting in the schoolhouse with a dozen people present. He established a Sunday school and prayer meetings, then went about to "cement elements" (gather future members) because "a church cannot now be organized to advantage."

literary society and local charitable works and in creating a settled atmosphere in their communities.

As mentioned above, another feather in any mining town's cap came with gaining the county seat designation, a solid step toward permanence. In the San Juan region, Creede, Telluride, Lake City, Durango, Ouray, and Silverton gained that title, and all have survived as such into the twenty-first century. The "crown" did not guarantee rule, however. Rico secured the county seat, and then the declining community lost it after World War II to agricultural Dove Creek on the western end of the county. Not only did this designation provide a courthouse to the town's "skyline"; it supplied additional business, as outlying folks had to come in for county or legal matters.

Sometimes a little political struggle was required to gain the honor. Durango voters took the county seat away from smaller and dwindling

With a church, a school, and businesses, a mining community was off and running. Mayday, at the mouth of La Plata Canyon, did not run far, its short boom arriving in the late 1890s. Remembering his Silverton school days in the early 1900s, Ernie Hoffman remarked, "If I got in trouble at school I automatically got in trouble at home. No question about that."

Steel millionaire Andrew Carnegie offered communities libraries. Silverton accepted, and in 1905 this library was completed, a sure sign of progress in locals' eyes. It has not changed a great deal since.

Parrott City. Silverton fought it out with Howardsville before finally winning an election. After the latter refused to turn over the county records, Silverton "stole" them, and the political focus shifted southward down the Animas River into Baker's Park. Neither of the losing communities ever recovered.

A varied business district, "up-to-date" architecture, a newspaper, and a church certainly placed the mining community on the road to Victorian acceptability. More was needed, or so believed these Victorians. A public school would help give the settlement an additional air of permanence and respectability. Eight grades appeared to be fine, but eventually in the towns a high school would be added. Not that most youngsters went that far in schooling, though a high school still showed the latest in educational developments and certainly would impress a family thinking of moving into the community. Schools, as mentioned, also offered the women the outlet of teaching, a professional one at that although a professional job did not guarantee equal pay for equal work, an idea several generations in the future.

Residents did not wax all that enthusiastic about taxes, but a city government proved essential to govern for the day and boost the community into tomorrow. Councilmen passed a variety of ordinances to solve an assortment of problems, needs, and concerns. Some proved dead letters on the books; others shaped the community. The ordinances often looked much like those that had been passed in the citizens' old hometown.

The community movers and shakers were usually well represented on the town council or board of trustees. Merchants, who had more invested in the stability and future of their town than their neighbors did, often dominated. The merchants might be joined by a mining man, a male teacher, occasionally a minister, a newspaperman, or a local politician from any walk of life. Barring political upheaval, they represented the mainstream, middle-class, white, conservative, Protestant majority that took it upon itself to guide the community's destiny.

Harder to define but important nevertheless was civic attitude. Mining towns exhibited it over the camps with their stronger mining base, larger business district, and other attributes. This attitude reflected a confidence, faith, and determination that tomorrow would be as good or better than today, which carried the towns through the booms and busts of mining. Mining camps tried to emulate that attitude; it simply did not fit well with them.

The city council and churchgoers often ran up against another fact of mining life: the red-light district. This entertainment section—saloons, gambling and dance halls, lower-class variety theaters, and cribs and parlor houses—was essential in the male-dominated, unmarried world of mining camps and towns. It provided an attraction that brought customers to the town or camp, helped them spend money, and "benefited" the community in a variety of ways.

The red-light district, of course, ran headlong into religious opposition and raised questions about Victorian morals and standards. Pressure came from all sides, sometimes overwhelming city councils. The contest became morality versus profit, a damned-if-you-do and damned-if-you-don't situation. More than one group of city fathers found a way around such a dilemma. Gambling, prostitution, and other "vices" were made criminal offenses, outfitted with a rigorous set of fines. Then they continued to be allowed to flourish, with monthly fines collected, resulting in lower taxes. It seemed as though the community could have its cake and eat it too.

It did not usually work out that way. Law enforcement expenses outran revenue, not to mention that the good folk might be tempted to indulge in the sin available in their community. To appease Victorian sensibilities and keep the "lost" from corrupting the "saved," the red-light districts found themselves placed in certain defined areas. Those who chose not to go there

In mining's masculine world, the red-light district remained essential. Very few of the cribs, out of which one girl worked, are left now. These are part of Telluride's row. Despite legends, working in the red-light district was not a glamorous life. Annie Grant, "one of the old time women of the half world," was judged insane and sent to the asylum at Pueblo, reported the San Miguel Examiner *on May 23, 1908.*

cast innuendos and gossip about those who did. A curfew and public disapproval helped keep most youngsters out of harm's way and from being lured down the wayward path.

Interestingly enough, the red-light district intrigued many tourists, for already by the 1880s, the mountainous West was attracting visitors. They came to see a lifestyle they were unaccustomed to back home and also the mines, mountains, and scenery. Sometimes they wanted to check on a local investment. Away from the restraints and neighbors of their hometown, they often sampled some of the other attractions available, things they might never have done back home for fear of public condemnation.

Tourists' reactions to the life and times of the mining West provide an interesting commentary. A variety of opinions were in evidence. Would-be miner and soon-to-be banker Alfred Camp, jotting in his journal, called Silverton a "burg" in 1875. While he appreciated the "great grandeur" of the mountains, he had some reservations: "One feels as if he

Cats had a difficult time adjusting to high elevations, but they, along with small dogs, provided companions for respectable women and also the "fair but frail" working on the line in the red-light district. George Darley recalled that one time a tomcat and a terrier dog "visited church," and "such a racket was never before heard in the choir corner."

is eventually (or so it seems) shut out from the rest of the world as there seems no way out." Silvertonians, on the other hand, thought of their community as a coming "metropolis." That same year another visitor, Benjamin Marsh, writing his wife on July 18, thought that "rents are high here" in Silverton and remarked that it rained nearly every day in the summer "and snows nearly all winter." Even so, he planned to stay. "Still I would like to make some money here if the show proves to be better than other places—I could stand it for awhile." That attitude kept the mining West moving for generations.

The scenery impressed mining engineer Eben Olcott. Commenting on a stage trip into Lake City, he wrote: "The scenery all along the Rio Grande and also in Clear Creek is surpassingly beautiful. Though I have been over it [the road] a number of times, it always appears more exquisite but it so varies as to defy description at least from me." Although an Episcopalian service did not please him—he was "very much disappointed in the minister"—a Presbyterian one did. "The service is so very pleasant that it is delightful to go. I wish they had two services."

"Look upon my works, ye mighty, and despair," wrote the poet Percy Bysshe Shelley in "Ozymandias." Tomboy ruins remind visitors of an American Stonehenge.

Harriet Backus's first night in Telluride did not endear the town to her. "Our cheerless hotel room contained a double bed. . . . Wearily falling into bed, we found the sheets cold and damp." A reporter, fresh from Denver in 1892, saw Creede as "the only place of the true frontier type in Colorado and it is doing its best to keep up its end." He did, however, see transformation coming: "A year from now it will have changed and the sober minded citizens will have shaped and molded it into an orderly town."

That perception of a "frontier" says much about what visitors expected to experience, to see and feel in a mining community. Even a person from the western town of Denver anticipated something unusual, as did eastern visitors arriving in Denver. The frontier image soon appeared in letters, newspapers and journal articles, speeches, and then books and

Far above Telluride was the Tomboy Mine. Around it were clustered the mine's and mill's industrial components and the miners' cabins and boardinghouses. Harriet Backus's Tomboy Bride *beautifully recalls life at the camp: "There was no kind of amusement for the men. For the miners it was work or sleep or occasionally rent a horse and go to Telluride."*

"Fade far away, dissolve, and quite forget . . .
The weariness, the fever, and the fret,"
wrote British poet John Keats. The ruin of
the Atlas Mill, near Yankee Boy Basin,
slowly returns to the earth, as does its memory.

helped brand the legend of the "frontier" on the public's mind. The mining community folk may not have desired that; they, after all, worked in the opposite direction to create a settled, civilized community and an image that reminded them of their own hometown and past.

This, then, is a thumbnail sketch of the San Juan mining communities. Like their contemporaries, they were part of the urban West of mining, a different West from that of their slower-paced, more traditional and conservative agricultural neighbors. They had helped induce the farmers and ranchers to come and conveniently provided a ready market for their produce and animals. Some remain, most are gone, but they left behind a rich heritage and the folklore of a bygone era.

The *Silverton Standard* (January 3, 1903) heralded the new year with an unsigned poem of six stanzas. Perhaps not the best poetry, the two

stanzas given here nevertheless express the pride of accomplishment since Charles Baker first sighted the park that bore his name, forty-three years before.

When Baker, from yon mountain top,
Beheld the spot that bears his name
He did not dream that here one day
A splendid city would acclaim
The riches at his feet.

And when the throng of eager men—
Men of heroic mound and true—
Wrought mines that silver might be had
They builded better than they knew
These men now gone.

Schoolhouse at Wagon Wheel Gap near Creede, Colorado
"In the country the repository of art and science was the school, and the schoolteacher
shielded and carried the torch of learning and of beauty. The schoolhouse was the
meeting place for music, for debate. The polls were set in the school house for elections.
Social life, whether it was the crowning of a May queen, the eulogy to a dead president,
or an all-night dance, could be held nowhere else."
—John Steinbeck, East of Eden, *1952*

Silverton was one of the earliest and also one of the most significant of the mining towns. Joined by Telluride and Ouray, these three towns represented the heart of San Juan mining for forty years.

SAN JUAN
URBANIZATION

A tribute to the double-jack teams that labored deep in the mountains is in Durango's Santa Rita Park. It is also a tribute to the region's major smelter, which once lay just across the Animas River near the coal mines that gave it and Durango life.

ℰPILOGUE

On a weekend summer day, Animas Forks may have thirty or more vehicles parked along its "main" street. Probably more visitors stroll around the site than those who arrived in the camp during its short heyday on a similar summer's day. Along the trails, where mules once plodded and ore wagons rumbled, ATVs and motorbikes now noisily intrude on the mountain stillness. Four-wheel-drive vehicles complete the "traffic jams" competing for the narrow right-of-way. Welcome to the twenty-first-century summer San Juans.

To alleviate traffic confrontations, Lake City jeep renters are rumored to actually pilot their customers one way over the Engineer and Cinnamon passes in the morning and the other way in the afternoon. What excitement these San Juans are to all those flatlanders who have never driven in the mountains but now navigate in their rented four-wheelers amid the peaks. Some wish they had never ventured forth; others drive with aplomb, hardly warranted by their experience.

Observing all this, one might honestly wonder if the majority of the tourists really understand what transpired here and grasp what the remains have to tell us. Some folks obviously are here simply to test their mountain rigs against the rugged trails. Others just as clearly did not know what they were in for and are hurrying to try to find the easiest way, hopefully the safest, back to "civilization." A few arrive in vehicles unsuited for the roads and trails, creating wonderment about what they were thinking, if they were indeed thinking.

For most, the scenery presents an awesome memory. For some, who take the time to look and contemplate about what they see of man's puny efforts to settle and work in these mountains, the trip takes on a deeper meaning. Optimistically, all take home a new appreciation of the San Juans and of the pioneers who tested themselves against these mountains while lusting for the silver and the gold hidden in their depths.

The ruins of the Tabasco Mill frame the American Basin. Miners generations ago dug to release the gold and silver from the granite depths of these mountains. Now silence has returned.

Nineteenth-century San Juaners would have appreciated, at least, that they had not been forgotten. For them, perhaps, they would rather that heritage had been more about their opportunities, their challenges, and their hopes. They were the ones who first tested these mountains, hoping to match their dreams against nature's reality and an unforgiving environment. To return to Dave Lavender in *Red Mountain*, one of his characters, Walt, suggests a rationale for why the old-time San Juaners came, stayed, and worked to an easterner, who looked about and could not comprehend the motivations or the circumstances that brought them and kept them in these mountains:

> But it wasn't the great wonderful mysterious secret you'd like
> to think it was. What made them go was a sort of urge, a
> frame of mind. One man that had it would take it up the hill
> with him and work his guts out, while the fellow next door

with the same feeling would use it sitting on his ass scheming out ways to cheat the first one. That's what built Red Mountain—the frame of mind of the people.

For us in the twenty-first century, in a far-distant time not measured solely by years, the above rationale might seem logical. But at the same time life in the mines or in a mining camp or town could appear a waste of time, talent, energy, and money for the limited returns most of the miners took home. Regardless of one's opinion, the story of the opening and settlement of the San Juans has Homeric hues. The settlement of the American West has become America's national legend.

What remains amid the hillsides and mountain valleys offers a glimpse of what transpired in the generation following the 1870s unlocking of this rugged wilderness. Those remnants cannot hope to tell the

An era is disappearing before our very eyes, just as these clouds are drifting down over Yankee Boy Basin. Much of what existed there yesterday is gone today, and by tomorrow, even less will remain.

Perhaps the symbol for an era, the remains of the Yankee Girl shaft house stand defiantly against the march of the seasons, a reminder of what once was and people now gone. As San Juan native David Lavender wrote about his beloved home country:

> *Only a few of the old industrial and residential buildings remain standing. . . .*
>
> *Mingled with the wreckage are hunks of rusting machinery, tangled cables, and twisted rails that once had supported ore cars. Gray tree stumps abound. Dumps of waste rock run like scabby tongues out from the mouths of prospect holes.*
>
> *Because the rubbish tells of a bold and strenuous life and because it is associated with such glamorous words as* gold *and* silver, *it seems romantic. . . . What strange quirks of hope and stubbornness led people to try to put down roots in this hard, demanding world, so different from anything the majority of them had ever known before?*

whole story, and they tender only a few physical remains for the passerby. Standing and fallen, they will remain with us but a short time longer, as the poet Charles Kingsley reminded that very same generation who built the structures:

> How fleet the works of man back to their earth again;
> Ancient and holy things fade like a dream.

Another generation and most of what remains today will go "back to the earth."

Colorado's longtime poet laureate Thomas Hornsby Ferril wrestled with the transitory nature of nineteenth-century Colorado mining. He saw both the triumph and the tragedy inherent within the story. In his poem "Ghost Town," Ferril wrote a perfect epitaph for an era and its generation of Coloradans:

> Here was the glint of the blossom rock,
> Here Colorado dug the gold
> For a sealskin vest and a rope of pearl
> And a garter jewel from Amsterdam
> And a house of stone with a jig-saw porch
> Over the hogbacks under the moon
> Out where the prairies are.
>
> Here's where the conifers long ago
> When there were conifers cried to the lovers:
> Dig in the earth for gold while you are young!
> Here's where they cut the conifers and ribbed
> The mines with conifers that sang no more,
> And here they dug the gold and went away,
> Here are the empty houses, hollow mountains,
> Even the rats, the beetles and the cattle
> That used these houses after they were gone
> Are gone; the gold is gone,
> There's nothing here,
> Only the deep mines crying to be filled.

| Epilogue

For centuries, the La Plata Mountains have displayed the wonders of nature for those who would take a moment to pause and praise.

Brother marmot races through a busy, noisy
summer as he prepares for a winter nap.

INDEX

Page numbers in *italic text* denote photographs.

Ames Power Plant, 31–32
Animas City, Colo., 6, *50*, 52
Animas Forks, Colo., *7*, 57, *58*
Atlas Mill, *69*

Bagley Mill, *37*
Baker, Charles, 6
Baker's Park, Colo., 6, 8, 63
base metals, 27
Black Bear Road, *19*
Brunot, Felix, *9*
Bullion City, Colo., 51

California Gulch, *2*
Camp Bird, 22, 23, 24, *30*
Capitol City, Colo., 57
Carson, Colo., *52*
Cave Basin, Colo., 26
churches, 59–60
coal, 27–28, 29
coke ovens, *27*
Columbia, Colo., 52
Corkscrew Gulch Turntable, *14*
counties, 18, 62–63
Creede, Colo., 18, 25
Cunningham Gulch, *44–45*
cyanide, *37*

Del Norte, Colo., 20
Denver & Rio Grande Railroad, 13–15
Dove Creek, Colo., 20
Durango, Colo.: as county seat,
    62; hotels, *21*; railroads, *17*;
    smelters, 35, *74*

electricity, 31–32

frontier image, 68–69

Gladstone, Colo., 51
gold, 6, 27, *27*, 36
Gold King Mine, 25, 31
government, 64

Howardsville, Colo., 51, 63
Hurricane Pass, *2*

Kohler Boarding House, *57*

Lake City, Colo.: attractions, 55, 56;
    churches, 60; establishment of,
    20–21; nearby camps, *49*, 52;
    newspapers, 59; railroads, 15
Lake Como, *4*
La Plata County, 27
Leadville, Colo., 12

Liberty Bell Mine, 25
lode claims, *10*
lodges, fraternal, 57

Mayday, Colo., *62*
Mear, Otto, 14–18
Meeker, Nathan, *18*
Mexico, 5–6
Miguel City, Colo., 52
mills: Atlas Mill, 69; Bagley Mill, *37*;
    Solid Democrat Mill, *35*, *36*;
    Tabasco Mill, *76*
Mineral Point, Colo., 51
minerals, 11
miners, 29, 31, 38–39, 54
mines: Gold King Mine, 25, 31;
    Liberty Bell Mine, 25; North Star
    Mine, 5; Silver Lake Mine, 25;
    Smuggler-Union Mine, 25;
    Tomboy Mine, 25, *68*; Ute-Ulay
    Mine, *49*, *50*
mining: and assayers, *23*; base
    metals, 27; coal, 27–28, 29;
    cyanide, *37*; gold, 6, 27, *27*, 36;
    industrialization, 29–35, 38–42;
    ore production, 22, 27, 32–35;
    in the Plata Mountains, 3–4;
    resources, 10–11
mules, *19*

Neigoldstown, Colo., 51
newspapers, 59
North Star Mine, *5*
Nunn, Lucien, 31

Olcott, Eben, 5
Old One Hundred boarding house,
    44–45
Ophir, Colo., 15
Ouray, Colo.: attractions, 53, 56;
    Camp Bird, 22, 23, 24, *30*;
    development of, 22–24;
    railroads, 15
Ouray County, 27

Picayune Gulch, *28*
Pickett, Rev. Joseph, *61*

railroads, 12–17, 24–25, 53
red-light districts, 64–65
Red Mountain, Colo., 57, 59
Red Mountain (Lavender), 2–3, 76–77
Rico, Colo., *20*, 25, 59
Rio Grande Southern Railroad, 14–17
roads, 17, *19*. *See also* trams

San Miguel County, 27
schools, 63
settlements, 3–5, 48–51, 57–61,
    64–65
silicosis, 31
silver, 12, 21–27, 35–36.
    s mining
Silver Lake Mine, 25
Silverton, Colo.: attractions, 53, 56;
    churches, *61*; as county seat, 63;
    its beginnings, 6; its boom, 25;
    library, *63*; railroads, 13–15
smelters, 32–35
Smuggler-Union Mine, 25
Solid Democrat Mill, *35*, *36*

Tabasco Mill, *76*
Tabor, Horace, 15
Telluride, Colo.: attractions, *54*,
        56; and electricity, *31–32*;
        establishment of, *52*; hospital,
        39; newspapers, *59*; railroads, 15,
        24–25, *53*; red-light district, *65*;
        roads, *19*
toll roads, 17
Tomboy Mine, 25, *68*
tourists, 65–68
trams, *25, 31–32, 34, 38*

unions, 38–39
uranium, 28
Utes, *4, 5, 8–10, 22–23*
Ute-Ulay Mine, *49, 50*

Walsh, Thomas, *22*
Western Federation of Miners, 38–39
women, 61–62

Yankee Girl shaft house, *78*